It's your time to be crative!

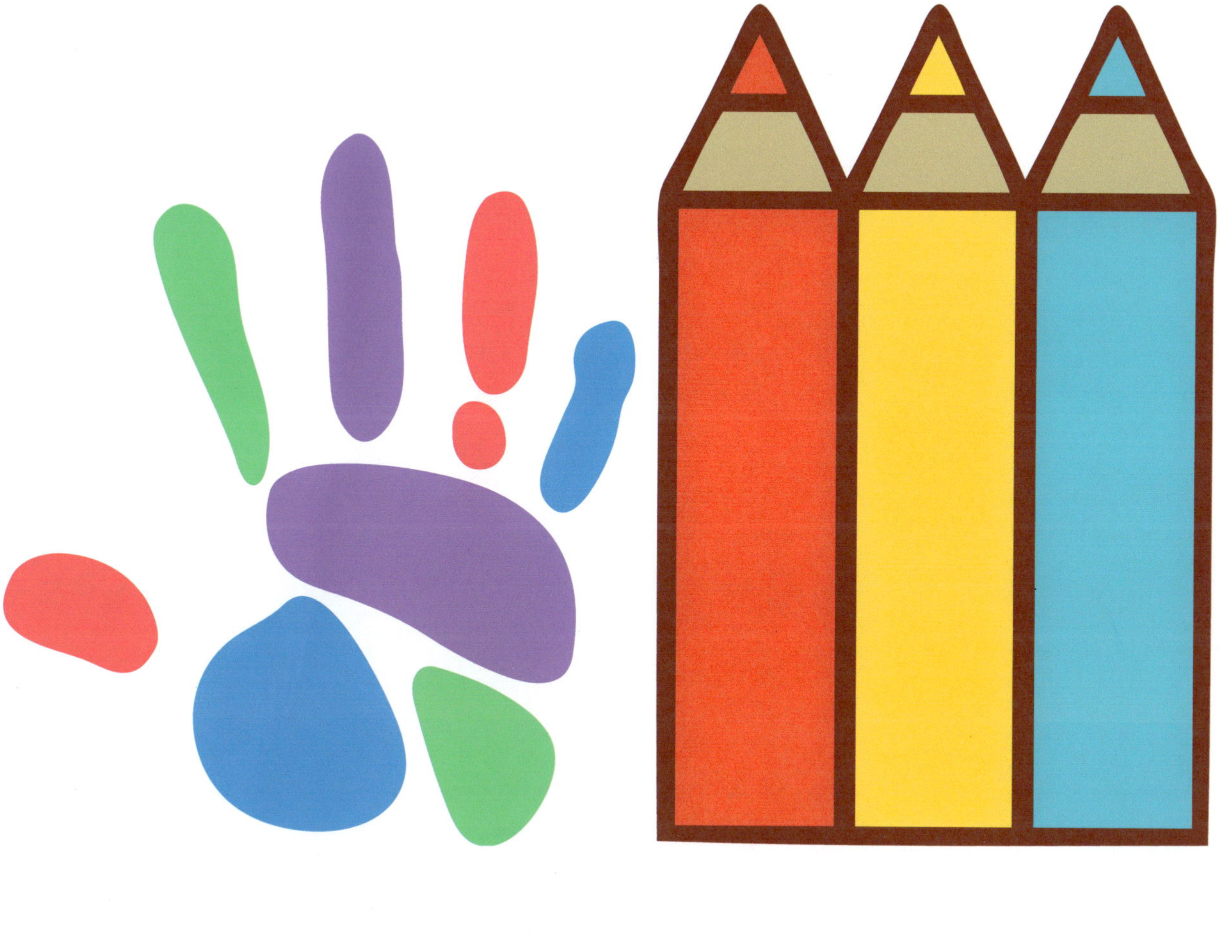

My name is___________

Let's get started

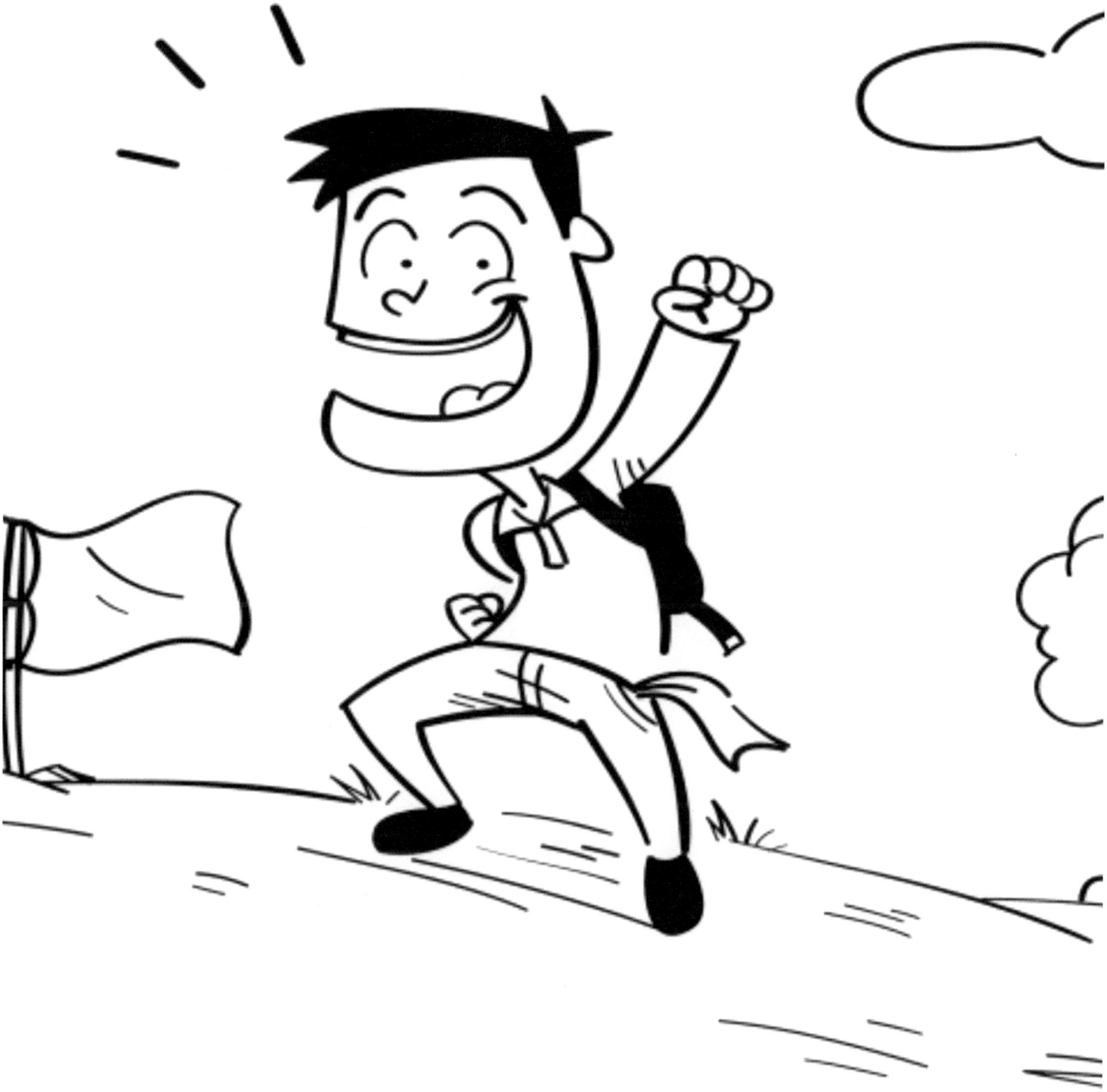

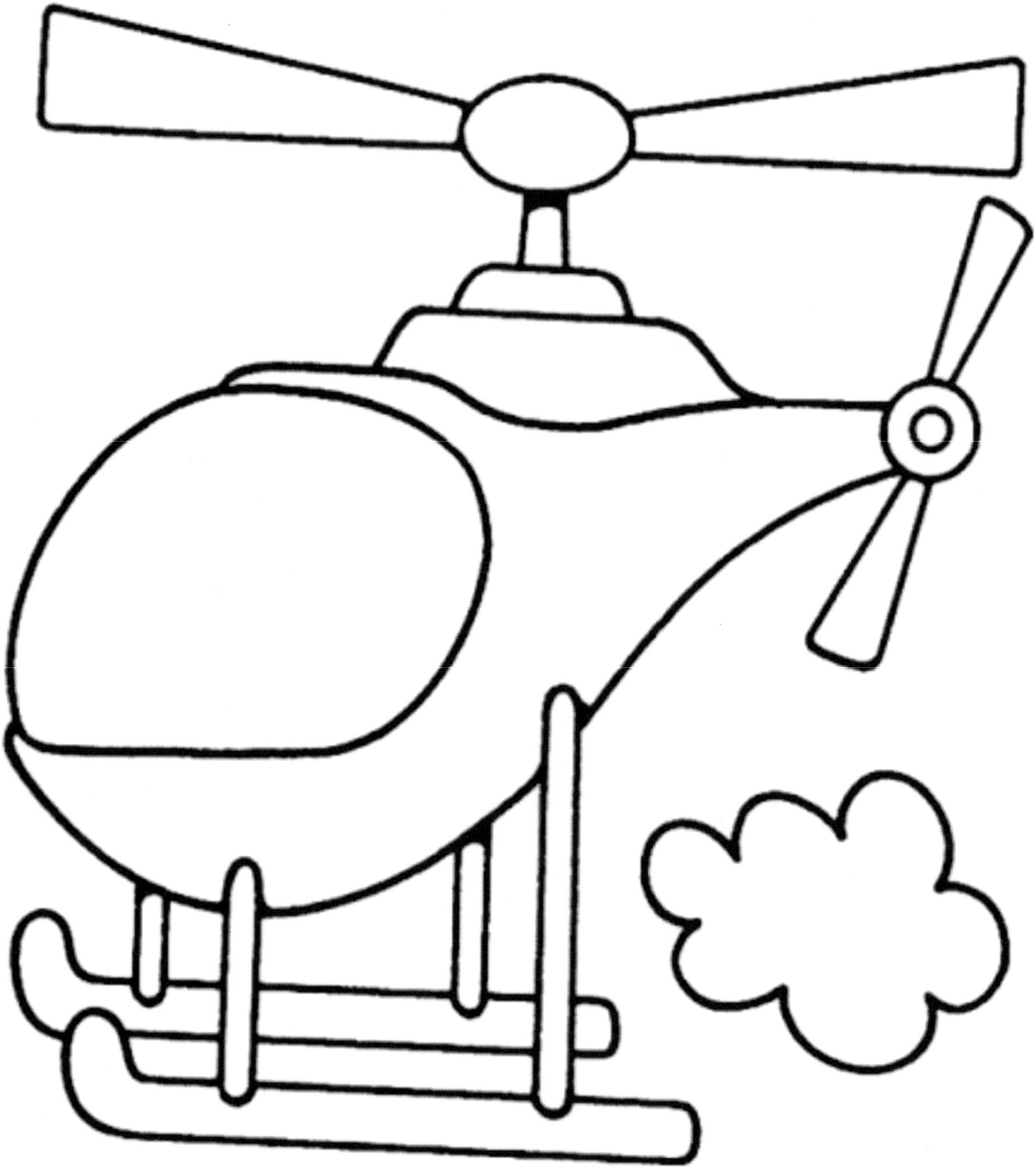

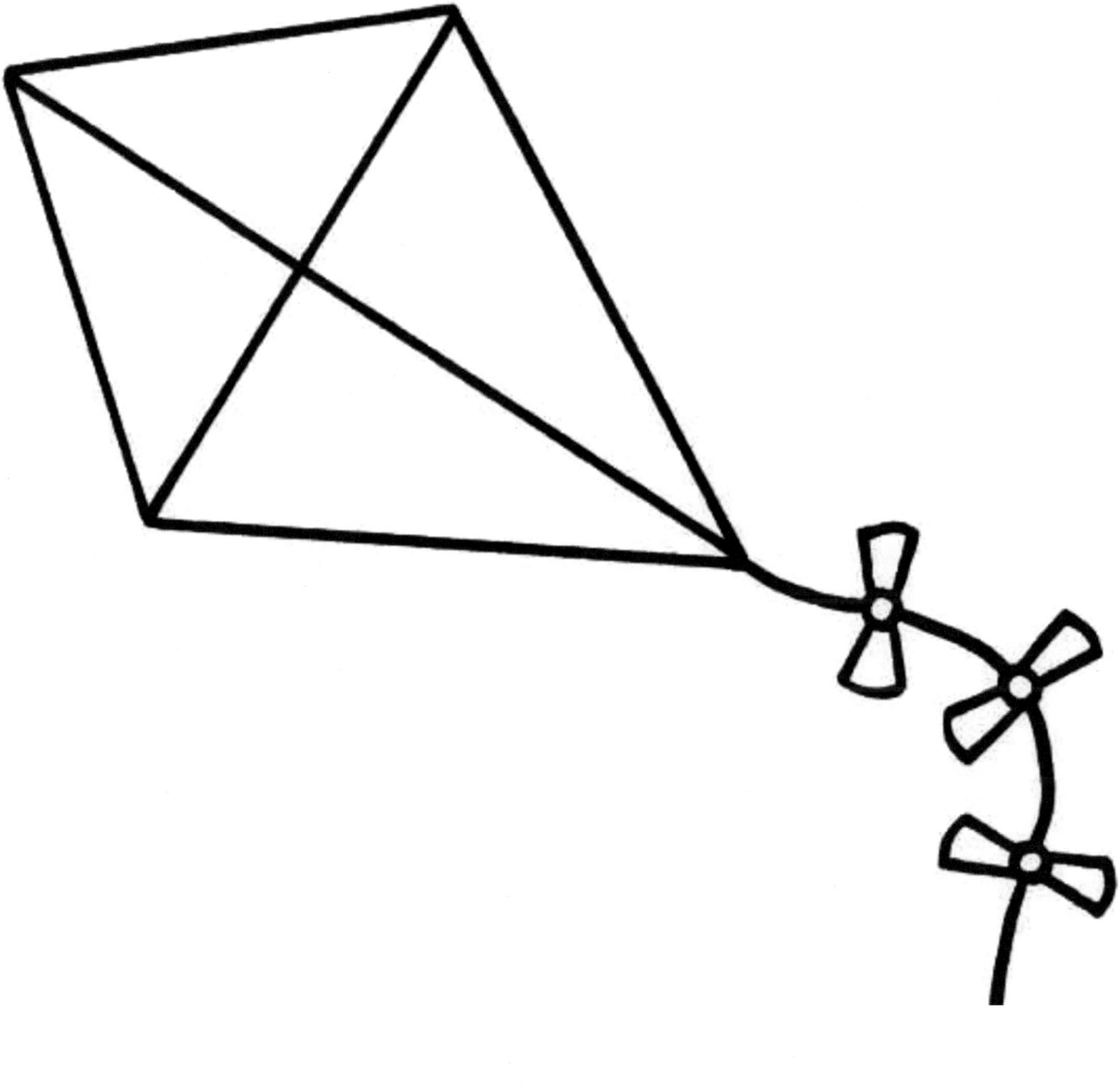

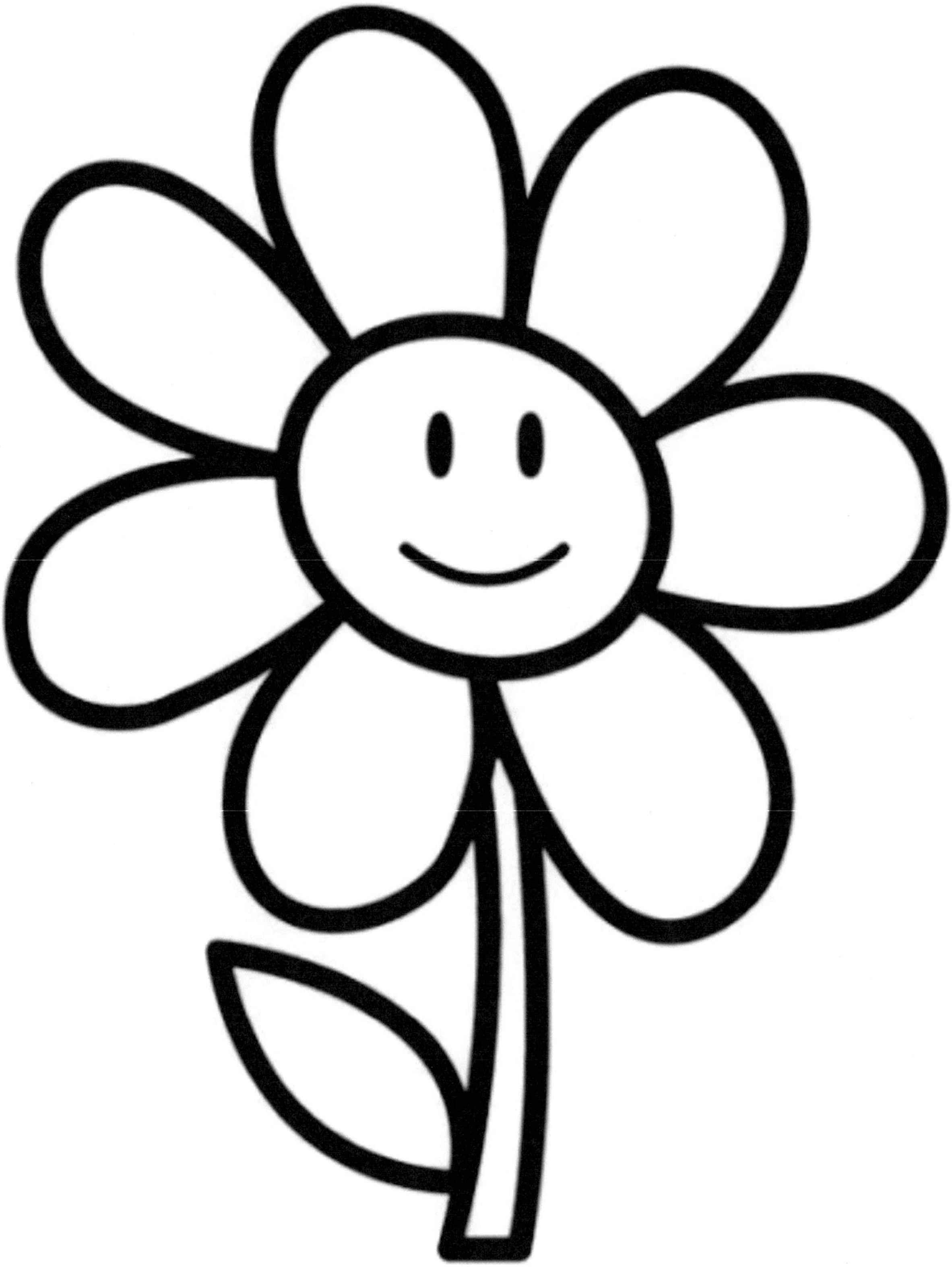

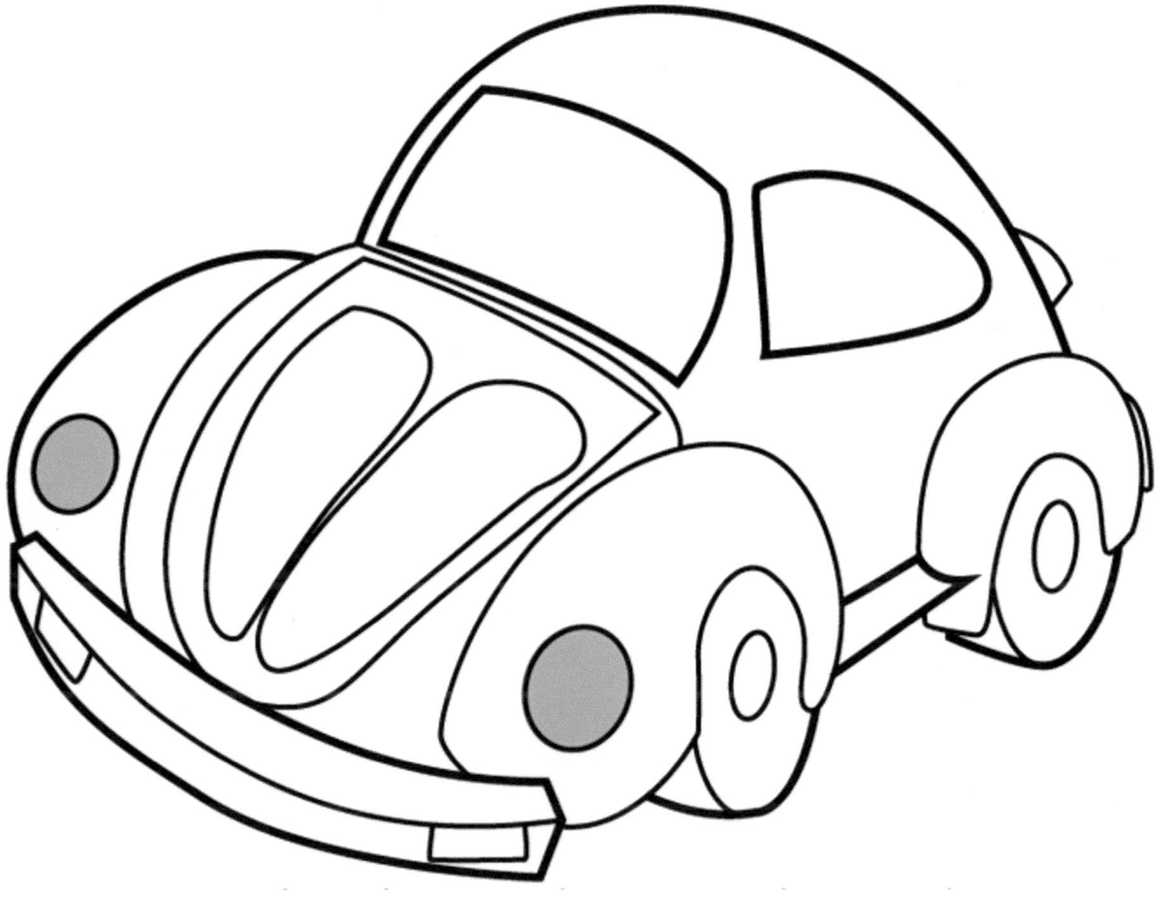

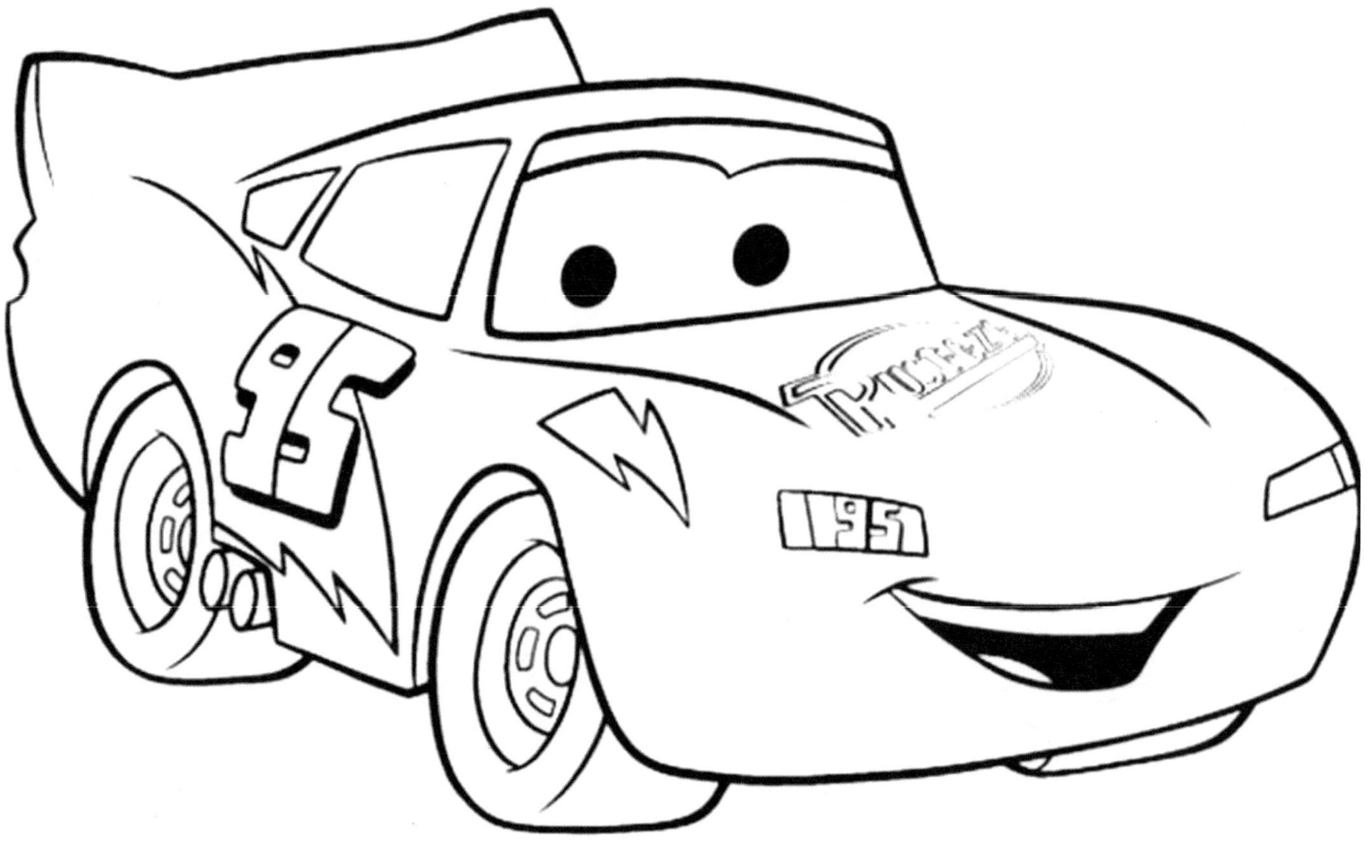
95

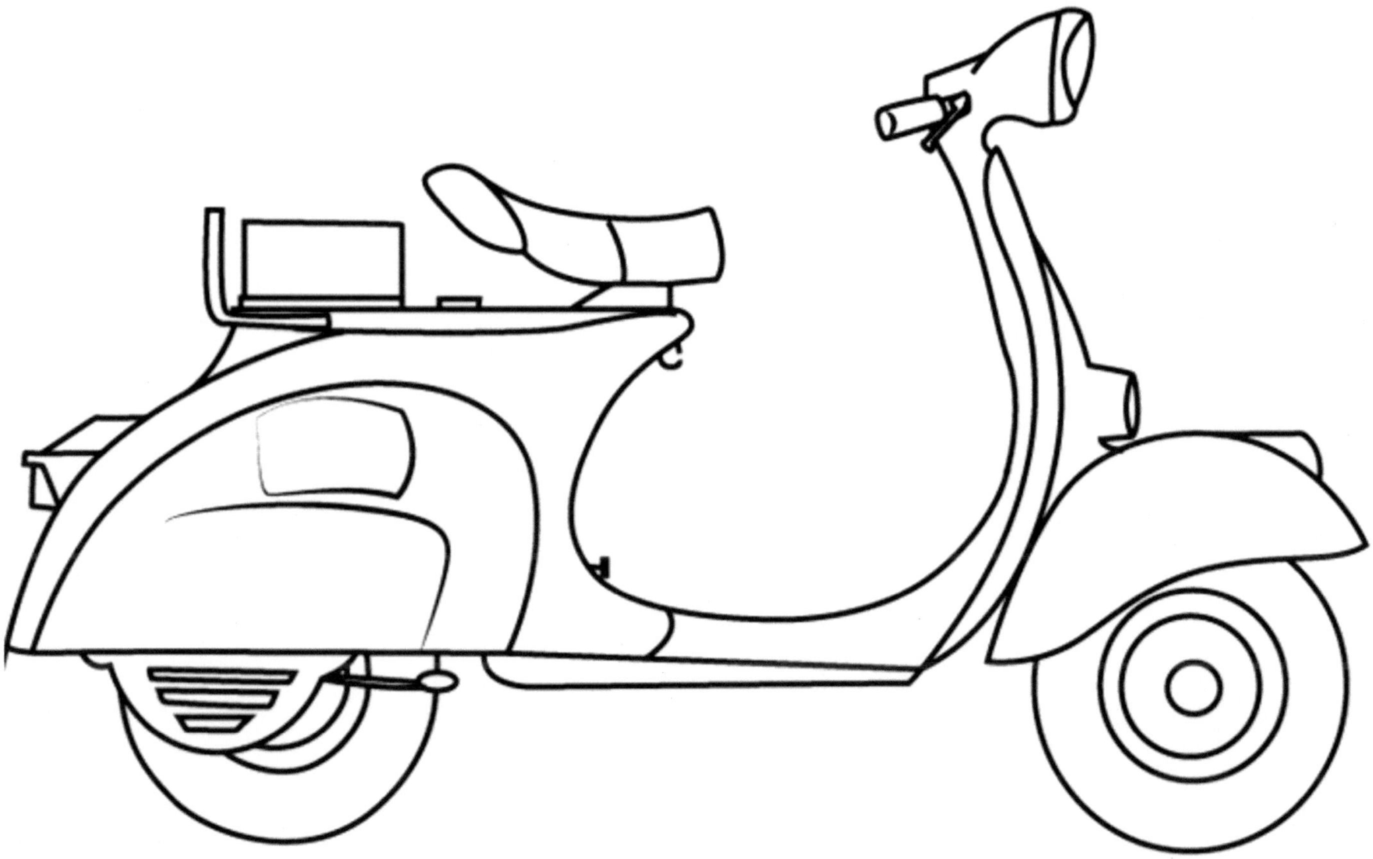

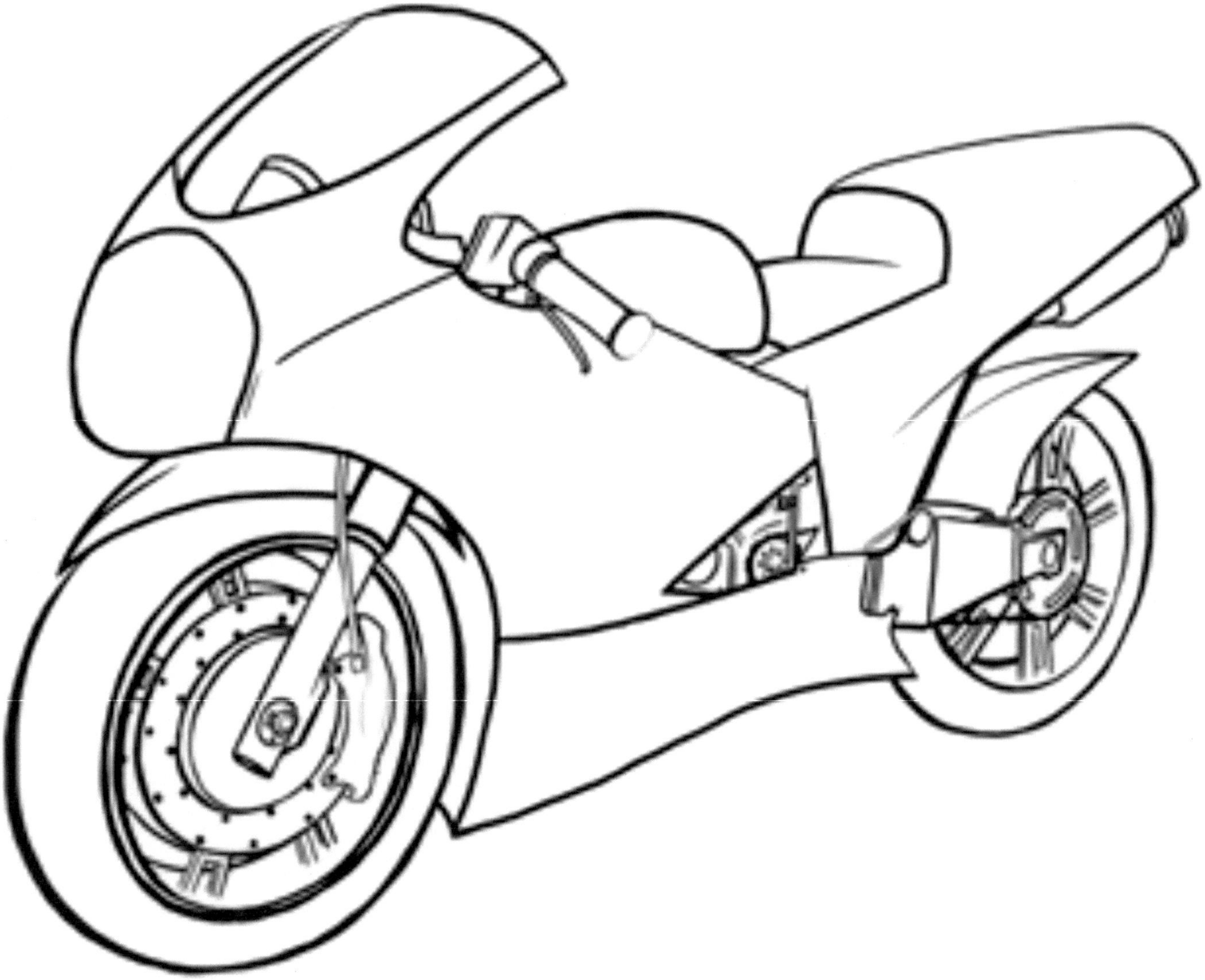

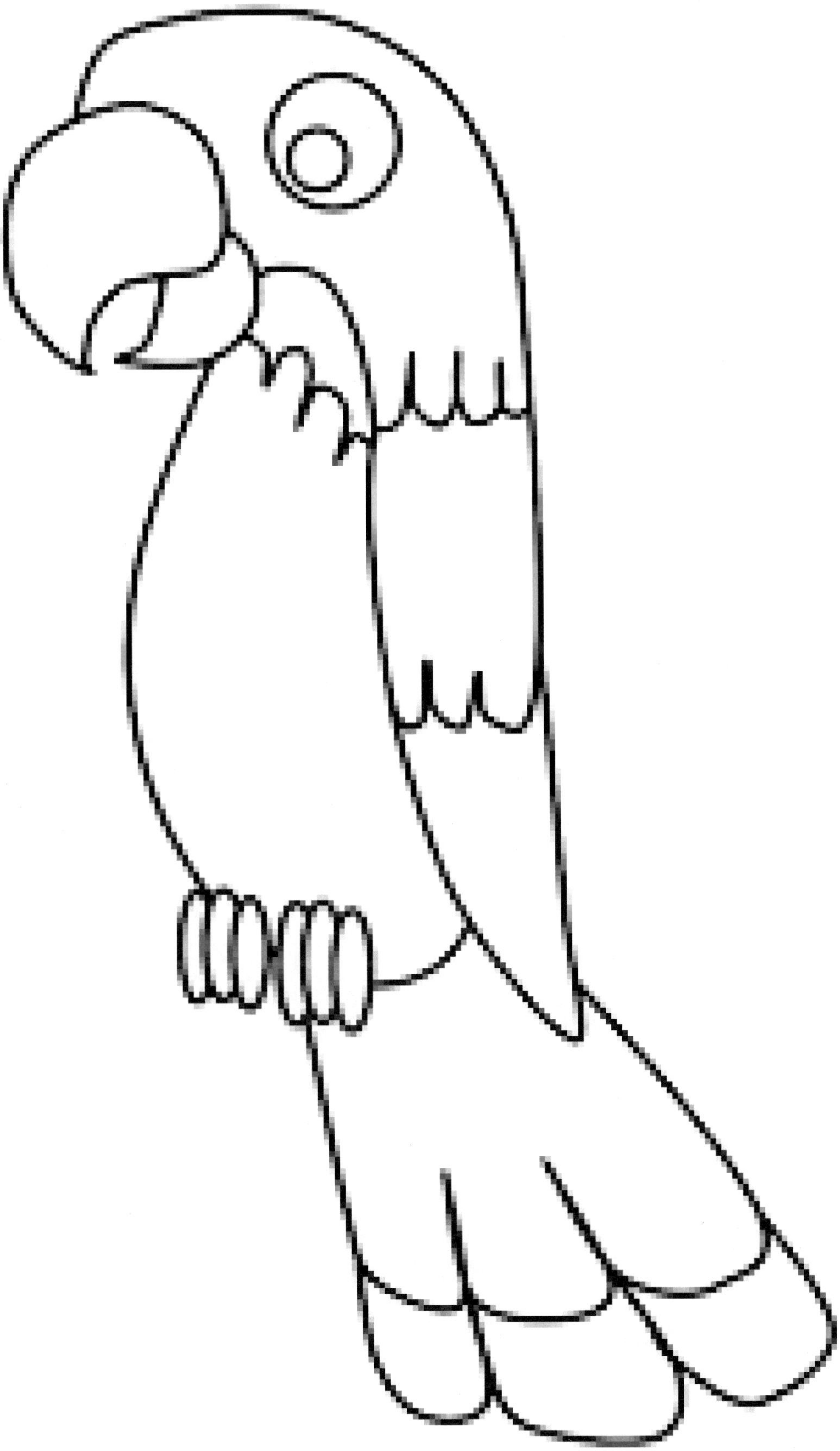

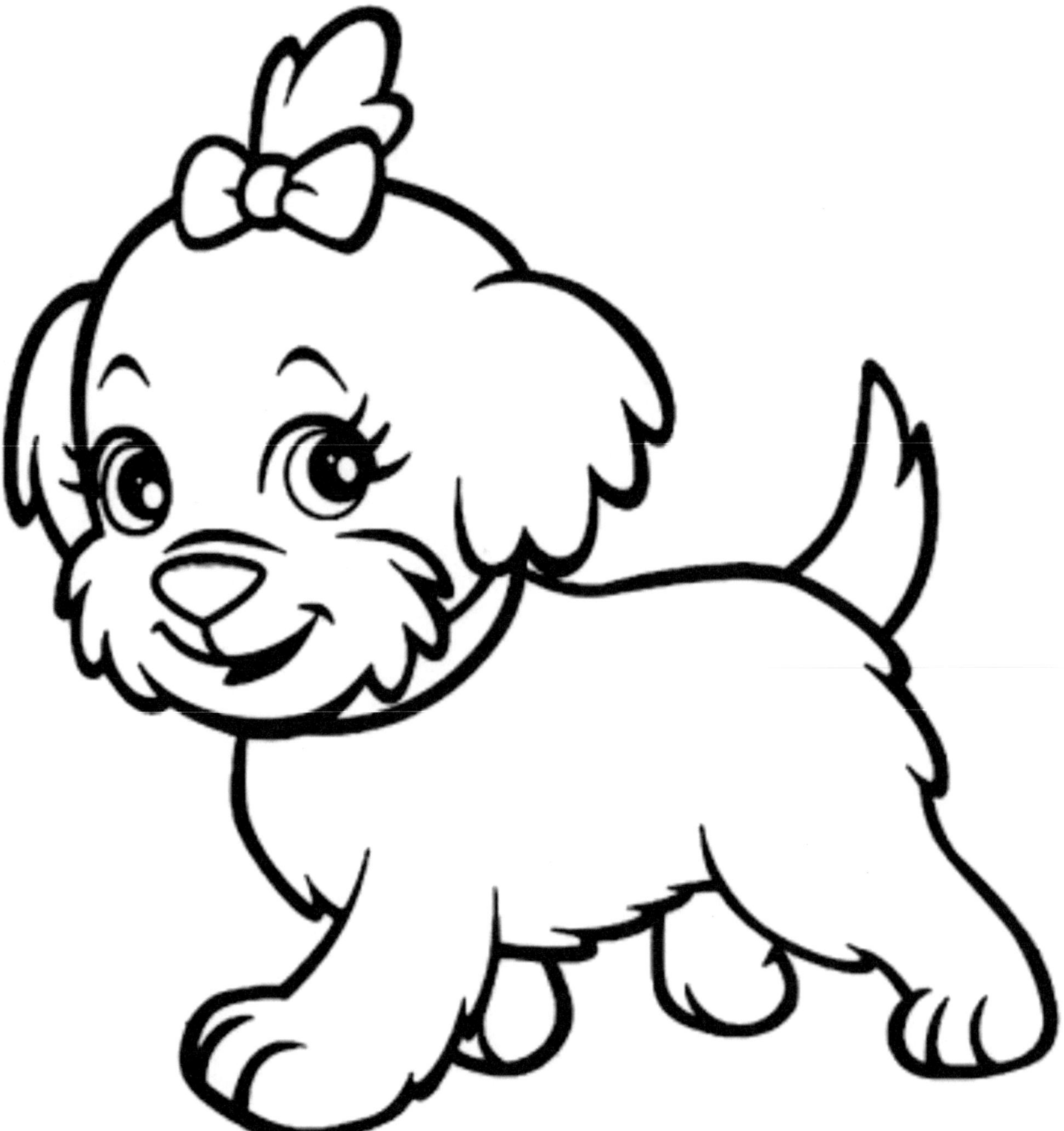

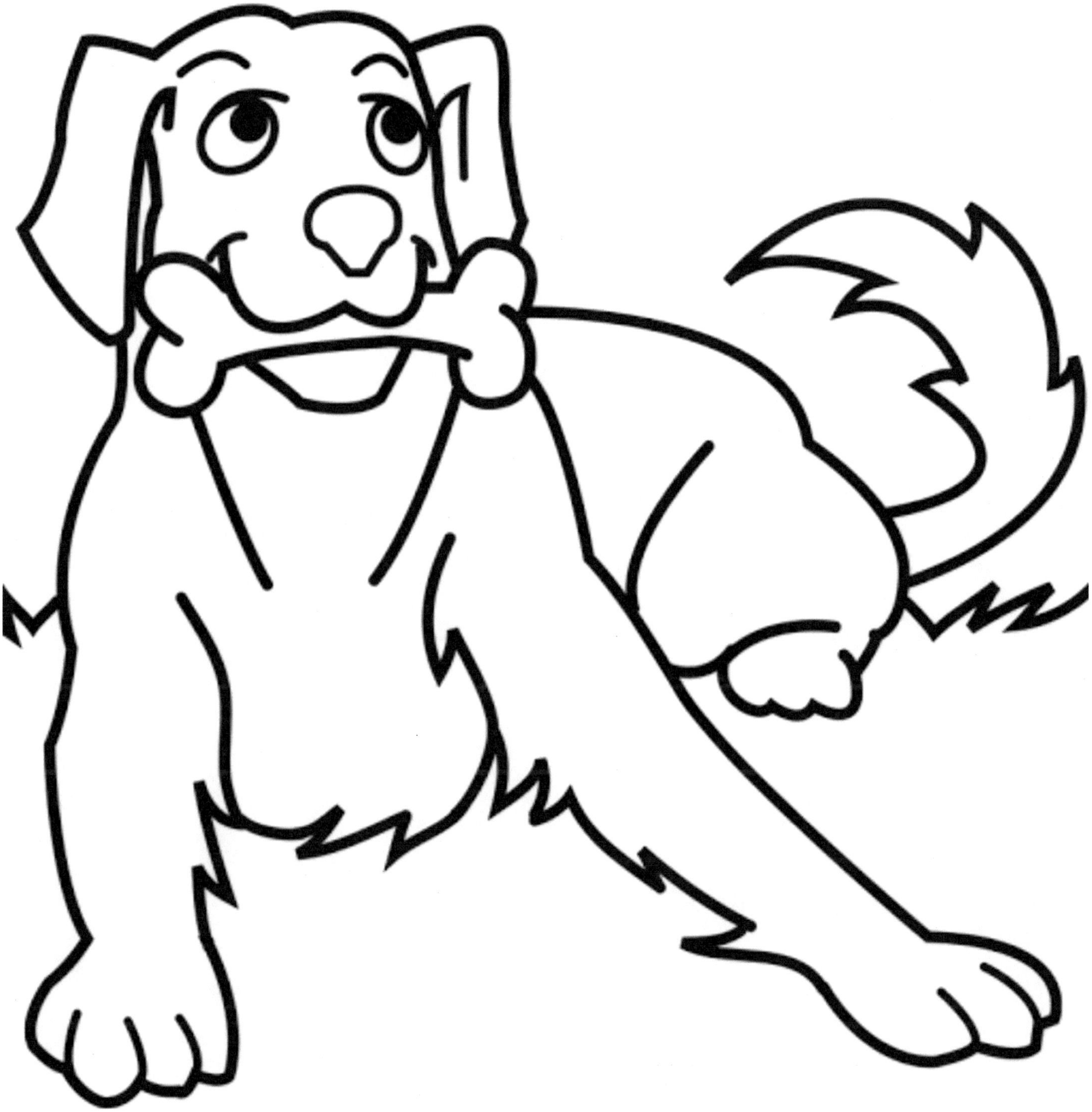

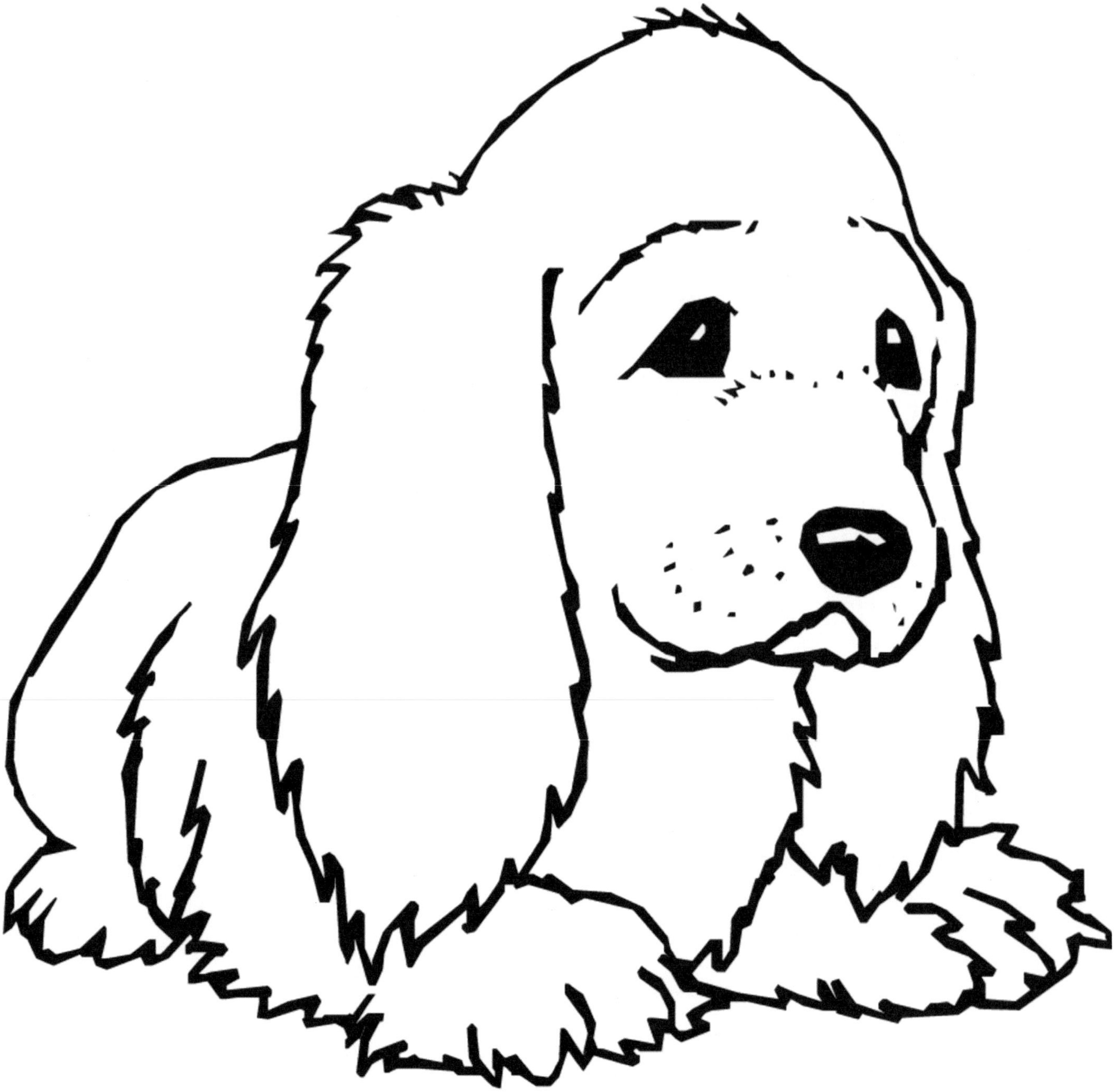

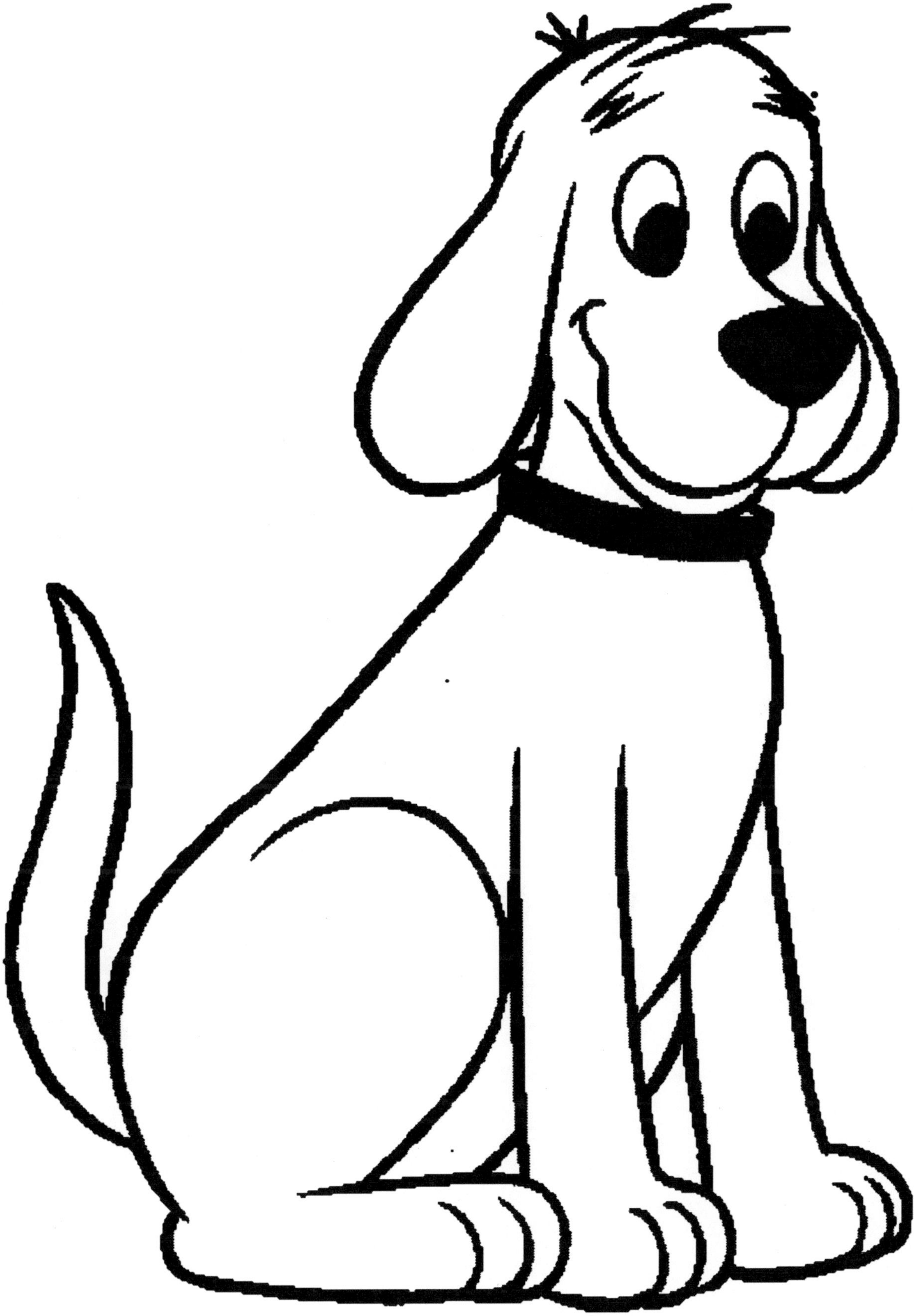

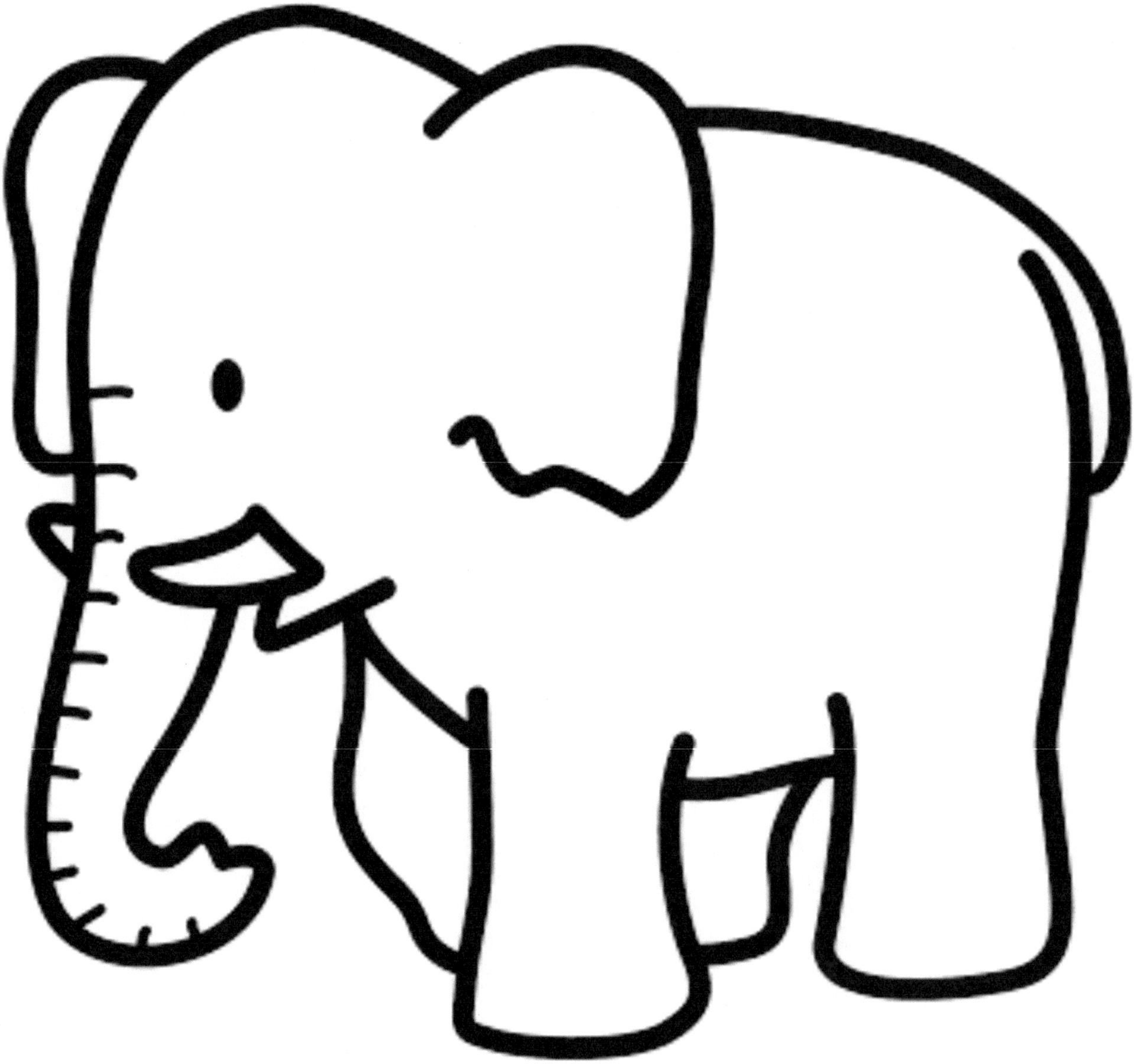

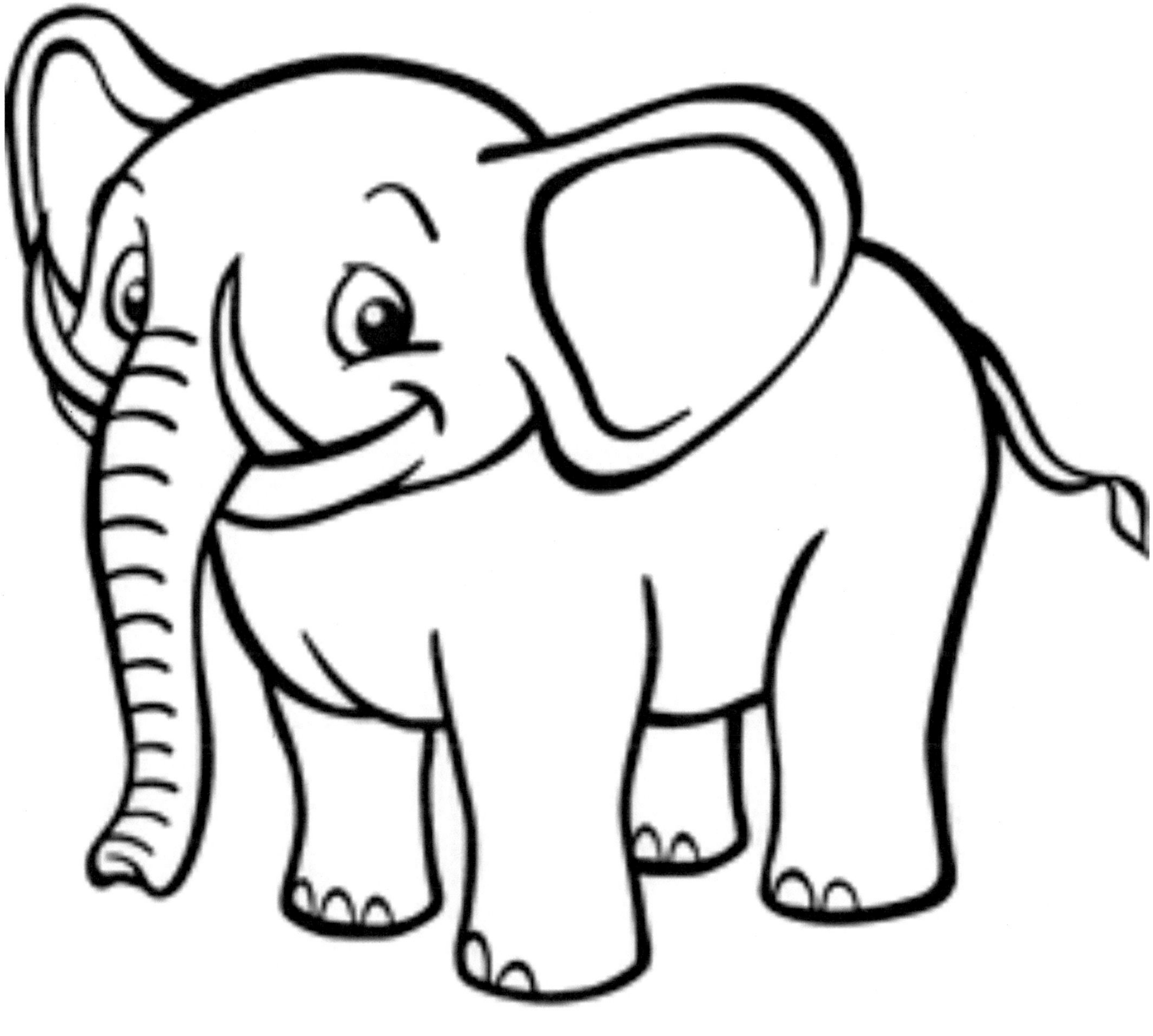

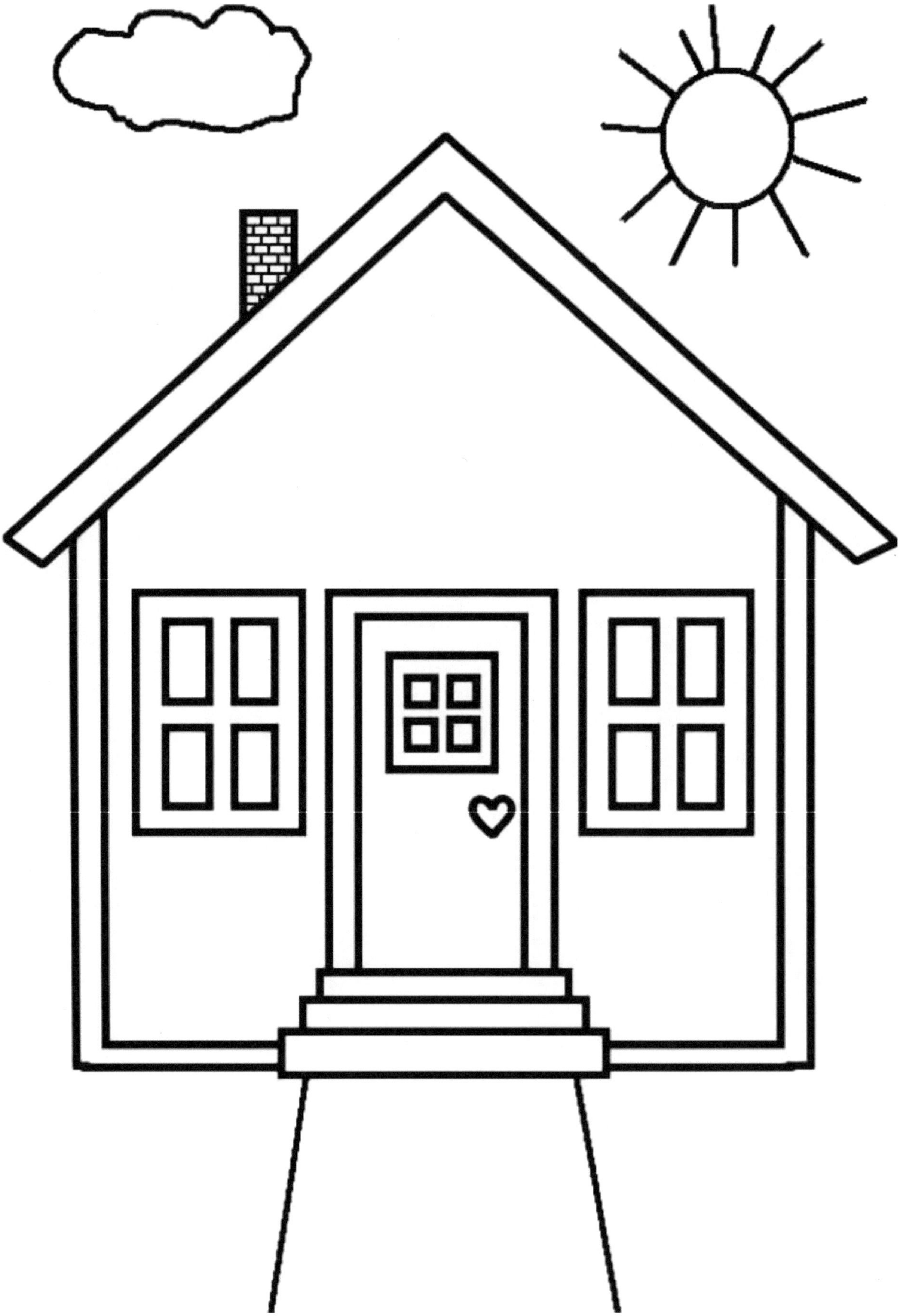

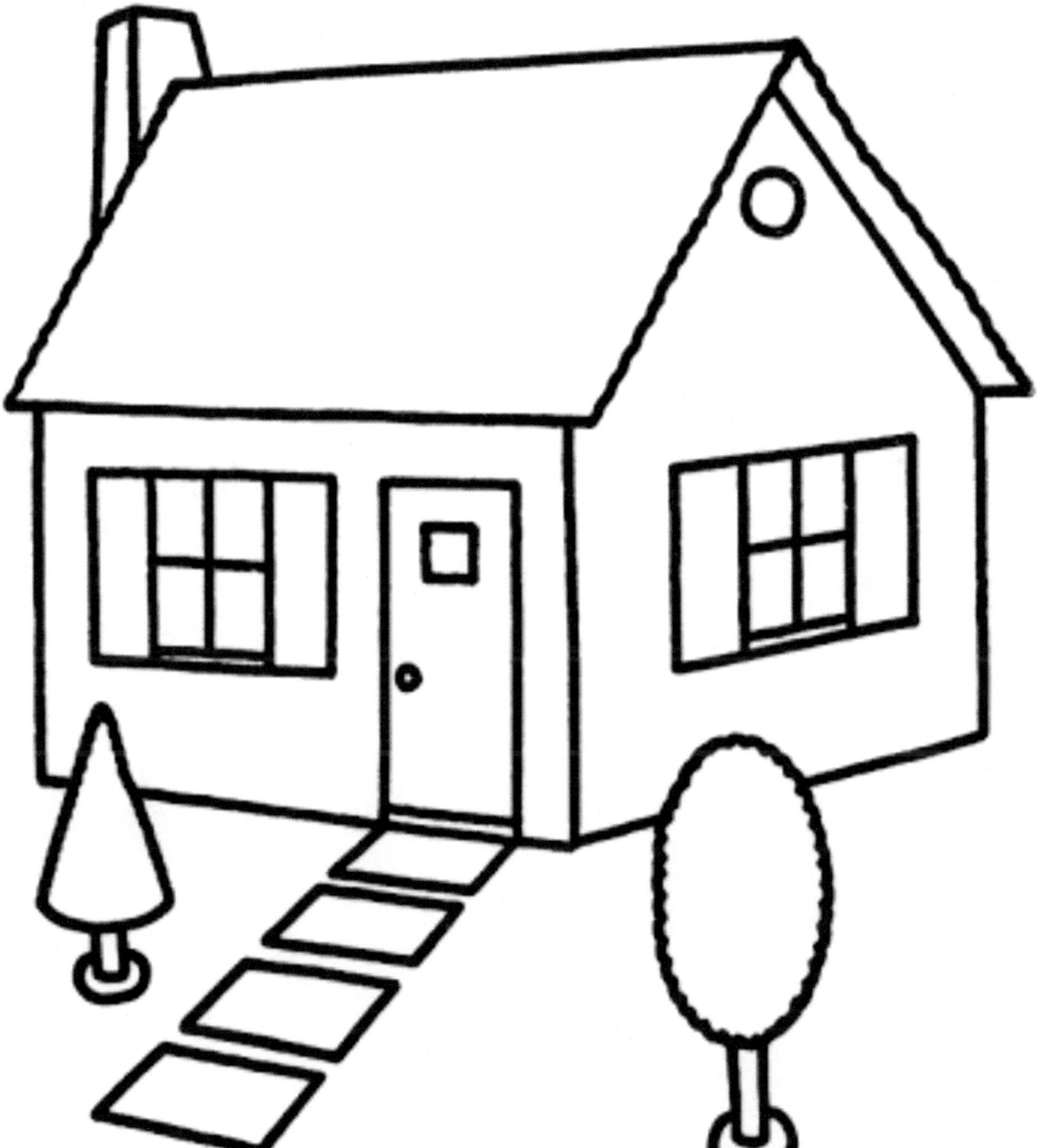

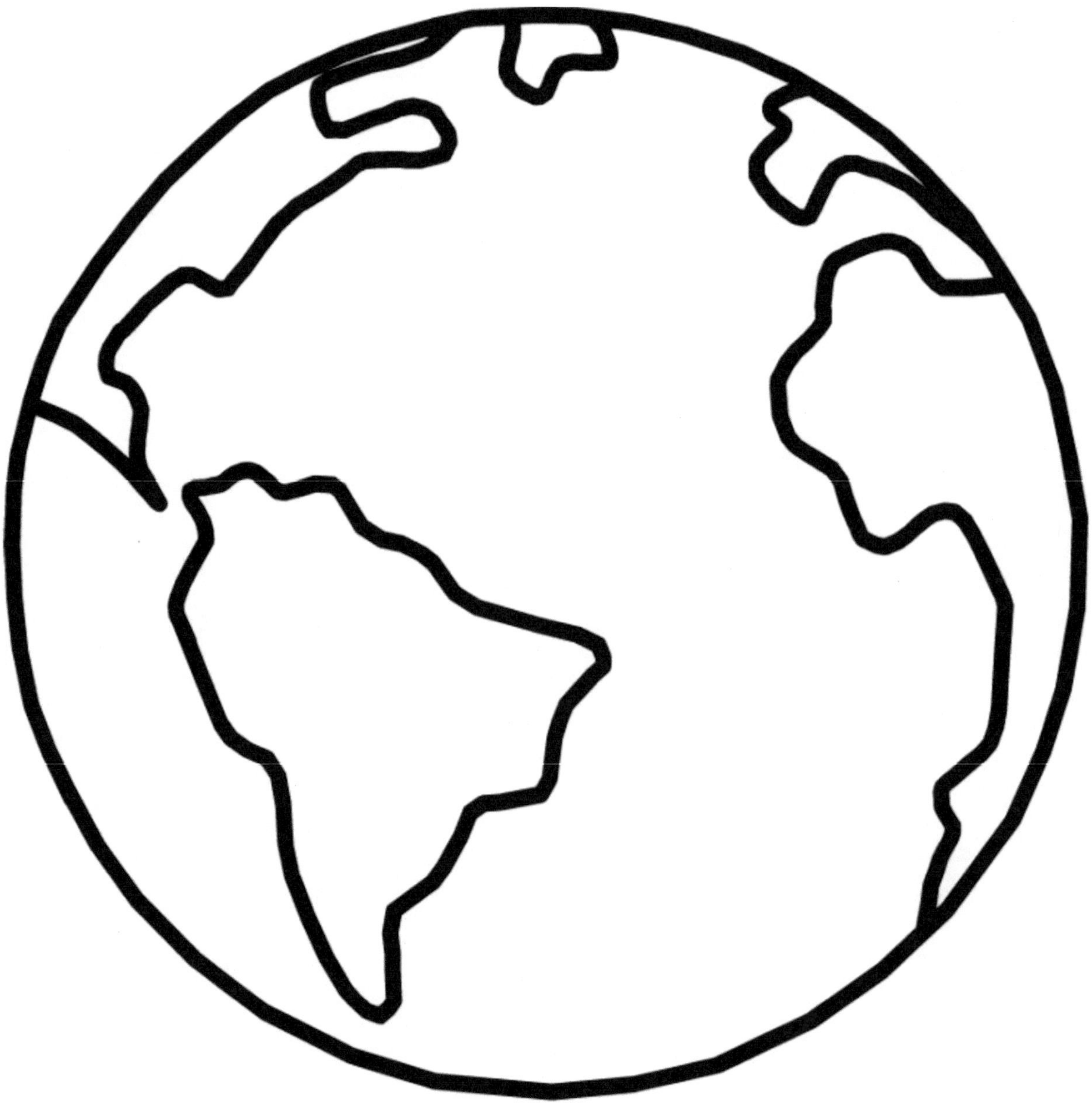

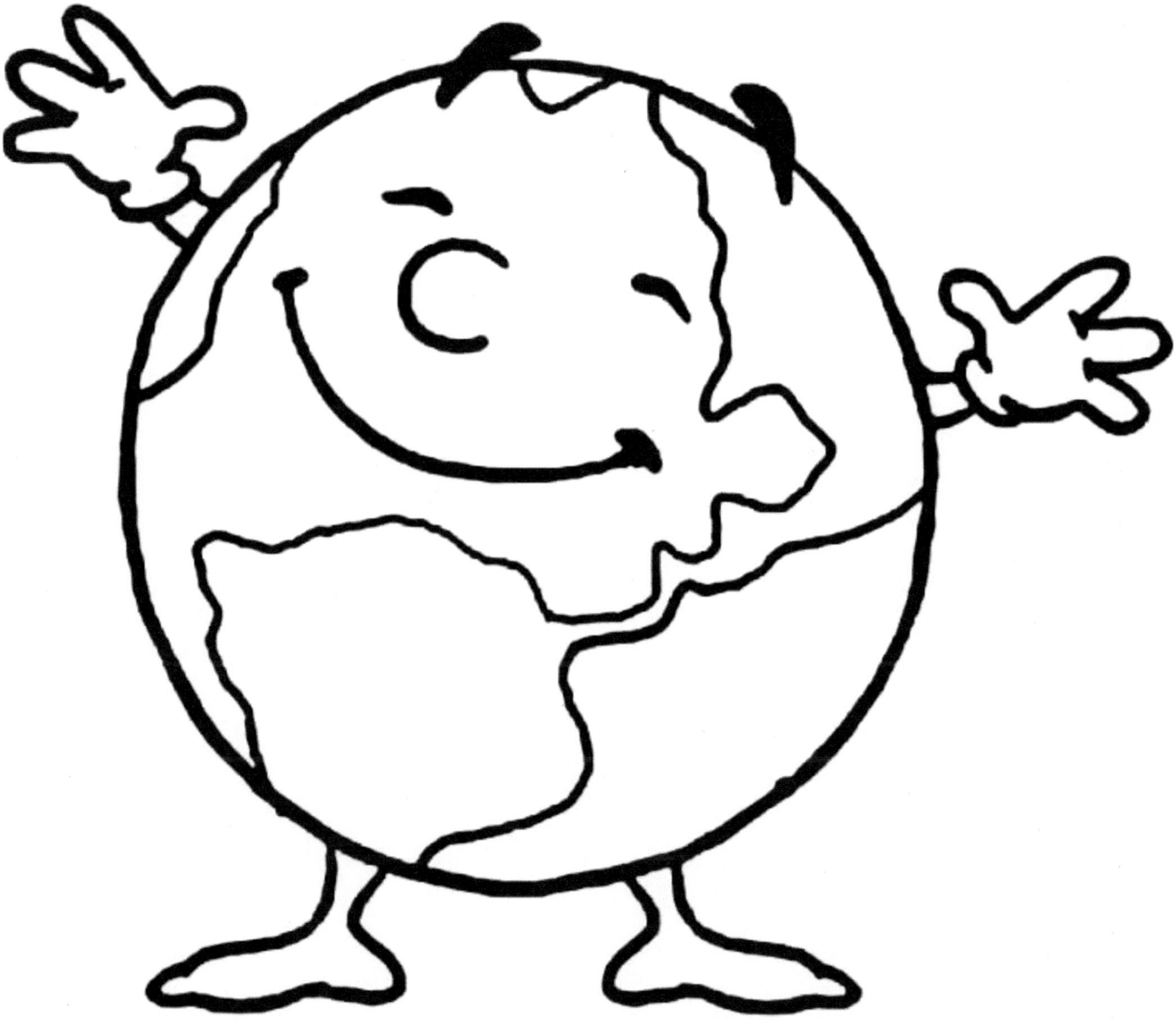

Here is some empty sheets for you to draw everything you want

Made in the USA
Columbia, SC
14 March 2025

55161530R00015